RADIO ETHIOPIA
TESTIMONY OF A DEVELOPMENT BRAT

TIM SHANER

© 2024 Tim shaner
ISBN 978-1-963908-19-0

Library of Congress Control Number: 2024943766

for Becky

Table of Contents

"Radio Ethiopia" 1
Elegy 15
Ferengis 21
Stuckside 47
"I remember." 65
Radio Ethiotopia 73
Acknowledgments 78

"RADIO ETHIOPIA"

"A guest is at first like gold, then later like silver, still later like common metal."

Amharic Proverb

When I first embarked upon this journey (grand tour), I titled it "Radio Ethiopia," not knowing that Patti Smith had titled her second album *Radio Ethiopia* and that my title had thus been taken. But even after I discovered that Patti Smith had *stolen* my title for the book I planned to write those many thirty years ago, thirty years or so ago, I was not dejected, figuring that, at the time, I had as much a claim to Radio Ethiopia as Patti Smith, because I actually lived there and, thanks to my father, regularly listened to Radio Ethiopia, making it so that, even though she used Radio Ethiopia first, that didn't mean she alone was entitled to it, not that she'd say that, I mean, for the record, I'm a fan of Patti Smith, in fact I'm currently reading *M Train* as we speak and loving it, figuring that by reading it I might find a way to write *my* Radio Ethiopia, inspired, as it happens, by her book's first line, "It's not so easy writing about nothing," that therein was the key to unlocking Radio Ethiopia, that Radio Ethiopia could not only be about nothing but also nothing other than the story of my failure to write Radio Ethiopia, given the many aborted attempts over the years to write it, but also, given that Patti Smith's album *Radio Ethiopia* is not always *about* Ethiopia, so too My Radio Ethiopia would not always have to be about Ethiopia but oftentimes actually more about America* instead, about returning to America* and having to blend in with my fellow Americans* while also being a "development brat," a repatriated expatriate, and how that affected my sense of being, surrounded now by Americans*, and so carrying that *burden*, if you will, like some kind of John Bunyan, My Radio Ethiopia "delivered under the similitude of a dream," as it were, "my dangerous journey . . . from this world to that which is to come," and so forth. And so, in the process of researching Ethiopia and Patti Smith, Patti Smith becoming part of the process of writing "Ethiopia," I ended up also researching poet Arthur Rimbaud, discovering that poet Rosmarie Waldrop had translated a book by poet Alain Borer called *Rimbaud in Abyssinia*, Borer's thesis being that Ethiopia, then called Abyssinia, was basically Rimbaud's final poem, even though no such poem exists, insofar as it was never written, just lived, the poem being the living of it. Later still I discovered that Ethiopian poet Solomon Deressa—who died recently in Minnesota, having lived in exile in The States since the early 80s—had worked as an anchor for Radio Ethiopia, and I wondered whether I had heard his voice on the radio when I personally lived there in person in Ethiopia. Deressa coined the term "Hyphenated-Ethiopian," a term meant to convey "the challenges of living in two different cultures," which, in the end, is what I discovered Radio Ethiopia would have to be all about, being myself, in the end, a hyphenated-American*, a hyphenated *white*-American*, to be sure, hyphenated, blessedly, by Ethiopia. Thank you, New Flower!

"Radio Ethiopia is the name of our new record and it represents to us a naked field wherein anyone can express themselves. It's a free radio, ya know. We're the DJ's. The people are the DJ's. When we perform "Radio Ethiopia," I play guitar. I don't know how to play guitar, but I just get in a perfect rhythm and I play, I don't care. And the people are allowed to do as they wish. If it's a really good show, there's like a thousand, 10,000, 50,000 people. 50,000 minds, 50,000 sub-consciousnesses that I can dip into. I mean, the more people submit and the more I submit, the greater show it's going to be, the greater we're going to be. I mean, I don't like audiences who sit there and act cool like this—"pfft"—because nothing's going to happen."

https://dangerousminds.net/comments/radio_ethiopia_everything_you_love_most_about_patti

```
            "How I Came to Ethiopia

            First we started from Calif., and"
            flew to New York at the night.
            Then at ten fifting in the night we flew
            to Rome. Then we went to Greece
            and to Ethiopia."
```

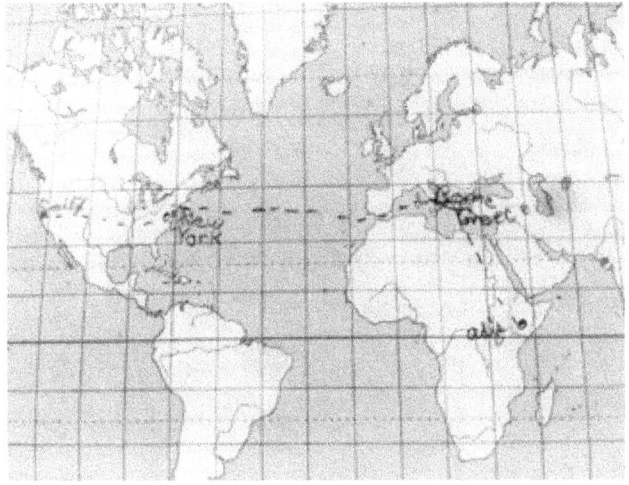

```
The main objectives of the contract were to:

1. conduct abroad economic analysis of the agricultural sec-
   tor,
2. help plan for a structural shift toward income producing
   activities in the agricultural sector,
3. select at least six potential agro industrial projects,
   and
4. prepare implementation plans for these selected proj-
   ects. The Mission essentially asked "where can we put our
   chips?"
```

from: http://pdf.usaid.gov/pdf_docs/pnadw072.pdf

Radio Spicer: "And you have to go into a serial poem not knowing what the hell you're doing. That's the first thing. You have to be tricked into it. It has to be some path that you've never seen on a map before and so forth."

"Radio Ethiopia"

Ethiopia saved me from America*. Thank you, New Flower!

Because of Ethiopia, when in America*, I didn't have to be American*. Of course, when we lived in Ethiopia, we were entirely American*.

Attending the American Community School, it was the only time America* had anything to do with community in my lifetime.

In Addis Ababa (New Flower), we lived in a compound surrounded by walls. Our horses lived on the other side of the southern wall, in a field between walls, though theirs were (on two sides) barbed wire while ours were stone from the quarry down the road.

Later, living behind walls in West Berlin, I was again totally American*, just as in England, I was American*, just as in Brasil, I was American*.

In Ost Berlin, too, I was totally amerikanisch, coming and freely going. Laughing at the guards in their booths. Stuck there. They, not us.

During Carnaval, my Brazilian friends used my status as an American* to get us into the cool club in town. They told the doorman I was American* and that this was my first Carnaval, so he let us in, thanks to me and my *country of origin*.

When we first returned to the USA, moving to Fort Collins, Colorado, my ninth-grade peers called me an African. I didn't know what that was meant to mean, and I suspect they didn't entirely either—*Africa's a continent you know.*

That I was a white American* mattered little to my white junior high school amerikanisch peers who half the time wanted to kick the living daylights out of me, me the African, yet they and me, totally white Americans*.

"How I Came to Ethiopia" is from *My Book About Ethiopia* (yellow folder, standard paper) which we assembled in my fourth-grade Amharic language class that was taught by a tall Ethiopian man dressed in a black suit, white shirt, and tie at the American Community School (ACS) in Addis Ababa in 1967. Some of the words in *My Book* are my own, like the words following the prompt "How I Came," but most of them were dictated by our teacher. Although *My Book* contains factual information, at a certain point the views of the speaker (our teacher), which flowed into the ears of his listeners (students), then through their pencils onto sheets of paper, bleed through, in particular his sense of superiority over people from the eastern part of the country:

Being his words, but written in my (fourth grade) hand at the American Community School, are my teacher's words my words too? Does placing them here make them mine?

verbs

nika – touch (b)
nika – (girl)
sif – write

verbs

verbs

zega (boy) shut
jige (girl) shut
kefet (boy) open
kifetch (girl open
ampta bring (boy)
amchi – (girl)
siteny – give me (boy)
sichan – (girl)
Kumi – stand up (girl)
Kum – stand up (boy)
tikumit – sit down (boy)
tikumitch – sit down (girl
nay – come (girl)
nar – come (boy)
wusrid (boy) take
wusrije – (girl) take
askumit B put down
askumitch g
anure B
anuri g

from My Book About Ethiopia

Poet Alli Warren's book *Here Come the Warm Jets* (City Lights, 2014), which is the title of Brian Eno's first (solo) album (Editions, 1973), brings to mind my proprietary dilemma vis-à-vis Patti Smith's second album *Radio Ethiopia* (Record Plant Studios, 1976). Thanks to poet Alli Warren, I figured I now have permission all these years later to use punk-rock legend Patti Smith's title as the title of my own book too, thanks to her, poet Alli Warren, but also because, as noted earlier, in living there, I actually listened to Radio Ethiopia, possibly hearing the words of hyphenated-Ethiopian poet Solomon Deressa streaming live from the radio in my father's Fiat, also listening once to the radio play of Hitchcock's *The Birds* there on Radio Ethiopia, at home in our house, huddled around the radio, listening to it in the late 60s, when everyone back in The States was *glued to the set*, watching the movie version on television, maybe, watching the war too, many sets in living color, streaming live through the screens in the living rooms, the war in living color and the birds and all that in living color in living rooms, the commercials too in living color, the birds between commercials and the war between birds between commercials, having as much if not more a claim etcetera, having lived there a good decade before Patti Smith took that title etcetera and made it her own—the album inferior, according to critics, to *Horses* (Arista Records, 1975), her remarkable debut, because it was too polished, apparently, with its heavy, self-conscious, self-indulgent guitars, a kind of failure, though heralded now as a work of genius—and for a good stretch of time, not just visiting, not a tourist, but living and breathing there as if it was normal, as if we were living our lives there, though not trying to colonize it, Dad insisting, as if we were Italians, or the British, not colonization, though Ethiopia was never colonized, the Ethiopians so proudly saying, unlike anywhere else in Africa, not trying to occupy the place, not living and breathing as colonizers but as Americans*, just trying, you know, to help, Dad more or less saying, and so maybe hearing the voice of poet Solomon Deressa streaming live through the radio in my father's Fiat, but then, even so, what's the big deal, right, I could just cut & paste that title as Alli Warren did Brian Eno's *Here Come the Warm Jets,* a title designed to be shared—"it's a free radio, ya know"—replacing this sense of owning, the result of over twenty years of exile in America* (home), twenty-plus years of the ownership society (imperial mode of living), with Ethiopia's collectivist sensibility, everyone there around the *mesob*, hands in each other's food, a collective ownership society (COS), our slogan "Just COS"—appropriating that from the Bush regime (Herbert Walker), the title of its invasion of Panama (Just [be]Cause), a test run for Operation Desert Storm (ODS)—let's celebrate it out in the open, one and all, let's come together, me, you, Patti Smith, Brian Eno, Hitchcock, Solomon Deressa, Vietnamese, poet Alli Warren, though not Herbert Walker & his brood, nor the Cheneys, they being out of the picture (i.e. not invited).

> Besides, it's poetry, so who's
> going to notice?
>
> Does Eno even know?
> Did she
> get his permission?

Alli Warren

hi tim! i hope you're well! i didn't really deal with copyright issues at all. city lights didn't mention it to me, and up to this point there haven't been any issues from Eno or his (ahem) estate (do people have estates while they are still alive?). i want to think this is because he's a cool person, but maybe it's just because he doesn't know the book exists. (Facebook)

> Radio Spicer: "And I think that the radio set doesn't really worry about whether [Cheney's] listening or not, and neither does the poet."

When Reagan got elected, I was more than happy not to be American*. But given that I left the USA at the end of 84, right after his re-election, flying first to New York (at ten fifting in the night) and then London and then on to West Berlin, I soon became American* again, which also meant that somehow I was also Ronald Reagan.

This reminded me of the time in Belo Horizonte, my first time there, in 76, when I met up with some of Simone's leftist friends, and we started talking music, and I mentioned some bands I was into, some art rock bands from England, and one of her friends, declaring his boycotting of Western music, aimed his critique of the hegemony of Western pop right at me, aiming it as if I was a representative of America* and Western pop in general, its erasure of the rest of the world, the world's music, though not so-called "World Music," "World Music" being Western music, essentially, and how it shoved out the influence of local music, of Brasilian music, in this case, and hence his refusal to listen to Western music. I, nineteen and *amerikanisch*, felt humiliated, of course, to have been put on the spot like that, feeling like an (fucking) idiot jerk or *ugly American**, though around this time I was just beginning to really like artists like Milton Nascimento and his *Clube da Esquina* ("Coração americano / Acordei de um sonho estranho") but also Caetano Veloso and Maria Bethânia and samba and later when I returned to The States, which was naturally depressing, feeling like I was in some kind of cultural wasteland, listening to that album of Choro and Egberto Gismonte's *Dança das Cabeças* and Geraldo Vandré, who, I was told, had been tortured so badly that he forgot how to play the guitar, and the others and then later Tom Zé and all that. But at that moment at the café, drinking beer with Simone's leftist friends, when Brasil was ruled by a military dictatorship, supported by the USA, at that moment I somehow was not Jimmy Carter, whereas when I moved to West Berlin and later London, I was definitely Ronald Reagan. In Brasil, for some I was JFK. For others, like Simone's friends, I was Nixon/Kissinger. But somehow, I never was Jimmy Carter.

At first I figured *Radio Ethiopia* would consist of a series of poems about my experiences in Ethiopia. And in fact I wrote a number of poems about those experiences and submitted them to a prestigious writer's conference, and through them, through Ethiopia, I got in, accepted because of Ethiopia. I wedged my way into the conference by using Ethiopia as my said wedge. I was told by my mentor not to expect to get accepted, as the conference was quite *competitive*, but with Ethiopia, I had a wedge.

"He chose your poem to workshop first," one of my conference peers said, "that's a sign." My mentor later saying, "As a poet, I'd kill for that experience." And so, me thinking, as such, that I was sitting on some kind of gold mine, the contents of my first book, the book that'd launch my career as a poet, a treasure trove, there in waiting. But then I happened upon Nietzsche's aphorism—"Poets behave shamelessly toward their experiences; they exploit them"—and I couldn't erase it from my mind.

Decades later, Radio Ethiopia remaining unwritten, I told my friend Chris of my conundrum, how I'd over-thought it, couldn't write it. I went through the history of it, the whole of it boiling down to the sense that in writing it I was re-exploiting it—the first exploitation being our having lived there. And so, writing it would be a colonizing gesture a couple steps removed.

And Chris said, "write that—"

Of course, you enter into it with good intentions, but being an American*, with America* right there behind you, all along the way, intentions, good or not, are beside the point. *Yes, but I didn't mean it that way. Those weren't my intentions.*

Radio Reagan: "I don't recall." "No, I don't recall hearing that." "I don't recall that."

"Radio Ethiopia"

Not having been able to write it, for so long trying, write about that
Because after all what is there to write, write about that
I wasn't going to go on about personal experiences as if, write about that
There was something special about them, about me, write about that
By virtue of the fact that I, an American*, grew up in Ethiopia, write about that
And so here, now, are the various experiences, what it was like, write about that
Chris nodding in recognition yesterday at the library, write about that
When I told him how Radio Ethiopia is about my inability, write about that
To write about Ethiopia, my exotic lifetime experience, write about that
I couldn't after all go on about my exotic experiences, I told him, write about that
As if just because I was in Ethiopia, and hence American*, write about that
My experiences were automatically exotic, exceptionally, write about that
Like when we played in the backyard and in the front yard, write about that
And how exotic that was, I wasn't going to say that, write about that
And how when we drove in a car, I wasn't going to say that, write about that
The VW station wagon or sometimes Dad's Fiat, write about that
And how exotic that was, I wasn't going to say that, his doors opening, write about that
Backwards, I said to Chris at the library, I wasn't going to say that, write about that
And how we went to ACS, the American Community School, write about that
Where I started learning Amharic, but they cancelled the class, write about that
And how we lived in a house with an alabaster staircase, write about that
And we had a maid and a gardener and a night watchmen who, write about that
Always fell asleep on the job, and who always bowed to us, write about that
When he came into the house to make the fire in the fireplace, write about that
And how we had Army privileges, and therefore could shop, write about that
At the PX and at the commissary and go to movies and play, write about that
Games at the Youth Club, watching movies like *The Green Berets*, write about that
And *The Mad Mad Mad Mad Mad World* and *The French Connection*, write about that
Or how I learned to play golf in Ethiopia, how exotic was that, write about that
I wasn't going to say that, and how I got a hole in one, twice, write about that
I wasn't going to say that, nor how I shook hands with God, write about that
His Imperial Majesty, who was quite short, I wasn't going to say that, write about that
Such that he had a man whose exclusive job it was, write about that
To place a small pillow under his feet, so that, I wasn't going to say that, write about that
When the chairs were too high, his feet didn't dangle, write about that
According to Ryszard Kapuscinski in *The Emperor*, him saying that not me, write about that
Write about him saying that and not you, not you saying that, write about that, not me,
His feet not dangling there, due to his majesty's imperial pillow, write about that, not me

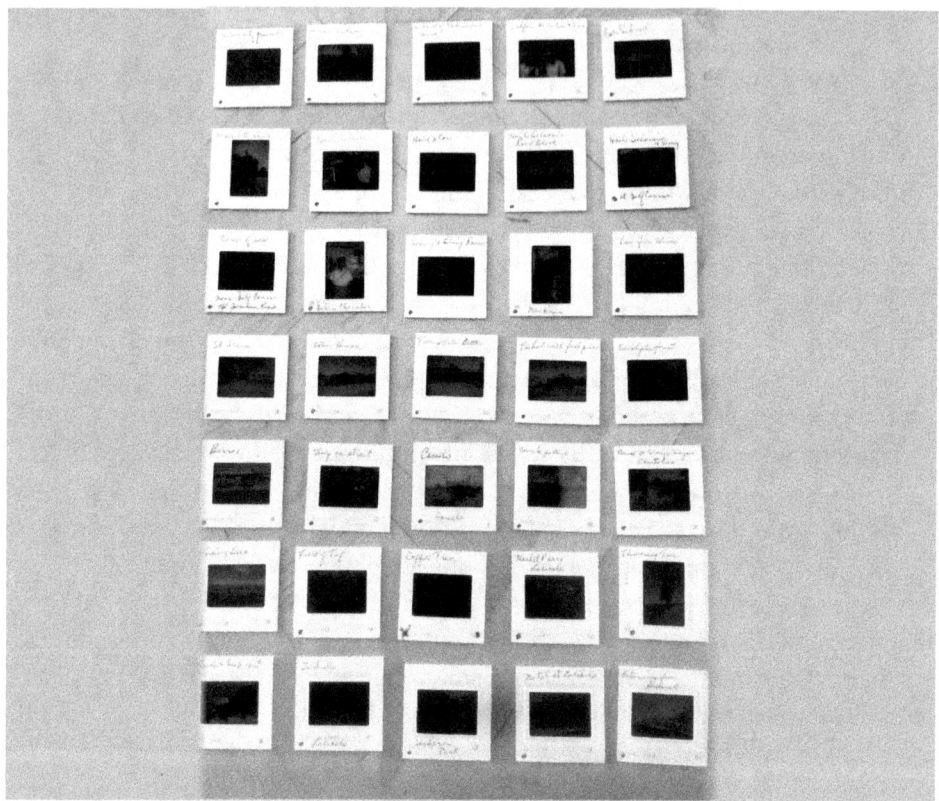

Grandad's Slides from Ethiopia Trip (1971), With Captions

Row 1: University Grounds, @ Amer. Embassy, in Front of Ambassador's Home, Welfare Director & Son, Amer. School
Row 2: Menelik II Tomb, Haile Selassie, Haile's Car, Haile Selassie Road Block, Haile Selassie & Sonny at Golf Course
Row 3: Home of Son Near Golf Course off Jimma Road, Gebre Christos, Sonny's Living Room, Mouk'ria, View from Home
Row 4: St. Scene, Native House, Filling Water Bottles, Tukul with Fuel Piles, Eucalyptus Forest
Row 5: Burros, Sheep on Street, Camels Camels, Cows to Pasture, Canal @ Wonji Sugar Plantation
Row 6: Farming Area, Fields of Teff, Coffee Tree, Market Place Lalibela, Flowering Tree
Row 7: Stools & Head Rest, Tukuls Lalibela, Soderay Pool, Motel at Lalibela, Returning from Funeral

ELEGY

"The daughter is like a bee for the family."
Amharic Proverb

I told her, not too long before her death, that when, twenty-four years earlier, our youngest brother Paul died at the young age of twenty-seven, stabbed in the heart with a kitchen knife by a fifty year old man he met just that day—"I'm going to kill him," the man saying, outside his friend's apartment, no one taking him seriously—I found myself thinking, cynically, how I'd end up using it, death lending the young poet a hitherto absent *gravitas*, walking up Lexington Avenue, devastated, disgusted, ashamed, the knife now turned in on me, walking toward Central Park then *in* Central Park, where, looking up at the blanched sun parked between the clouds, a sparse smattering of flakes drifting as if *forlorn* up there, falling up then down then sideways in a chaos of wind that, far below, scuttled dead leaves across the pavement…all these rehearsals coming at me like a bad poem, I vowed never to write it—

Later, not knowing where to go what to do, I headed back down through the park and stopped in at the Pace Gallery on 57th Street, where Agnes Martin had a show and, though I had been intrigued by her paintings before—hand-drawn grids over horizontal bluish-gray color fields—I had also been baffled by them, but this time, this day in which, at the office on Lexington, on the 37th floor, I received the news from my father, over the phone, "He's dead," its finality a bullet in the ear, on this day Agnes Martin was as transparent as can be, as if her paintings, and behind them the painter, were speaking right to me, right through me, and I thought for a while how I might write to her and tell her this story, but I waited too long—

SHE NO LONGER MOVES

"like a cork floating on a tempestuous ocean: he no longer moves,
but is in an element that moves"

Gilles Deleuze

Bare life running aside the freeway at 70mph, the eye settles on a fixed spot far off, but the fixture tears by in a blur of waves.

A trace of hills—far off and blue; some place you'll never visit; yet a place to live—as if you need be there.

Sitting, watching her, head on pillow, the tumors swarming her liver, not visibly apparent save her yellowish head, which wasn't as bad as I expected, strangely, not knowing before I arrived whether I could bear looking at her, seeing how the cancer was eating her, though mostly not in pain— she was calm, said, when asked, that mostly she thinks of nothing, other times of things still to be done, but I kept coming back to her legs, her hips, her feet, still healthy, alive, functional, as if untouched by what was going on inside, there to be used, ready to get up and go.

Back home, back home, back home, back home a trace of hills

Promising to go out into it more, regularly, to take walks, to drive toward the walks, park the car and then walk, the car in back, hot still & clicking, like a commercial in sunlight, its gaze the frame I'm in.

The letters she wanted to write each her children, but now out of time, before, in her illness, in the fluidity of, ten years of it, thinking she'd one day, a final letter to each, the words there circling, coming together, breaking apart, floating, things she thought she had time for it

She died a couple months ago, twenty-four years after Paul had passed, passed along, ten years after her initial diagnosis. I have the day written down in one of the two notebooks she sent me for Christmas. I couldn't help but read it as symbolic, some larger aspect to it all, that the day she died was on the last page of the second notebook. I was pleased by her gift when I opened it, thinking how well she knew me to have chosen them, the style of them. What I didn't know then was that the time it would take me to fill them with writing would be the time she had left to live. Yet, unlike the day my brother died, after I fled the office not knowing where to go, vowing never to write about it—unlike that day, I allowed myself to linger in the thought, to inscribe that day in the notebook, and then write, write it here

> For over thirty years now
> you've been meaning—
> Early on you were alerted
> to the treasure trove
> before you, the trove,
> the treasure, for the taking,
> extractive, as such.
> Nietzsche, etc.
> Shame, etc.
> Poets, etc.
> Why were we there, what
> Were we doing? His career,
> His life our life too:
> "What do you mean,
> 'Why were we there?!'"
> *I did not mean*
> *to say that nor*
> *did I really say*
> *that's what you're*
> *saying, right? No.*
> But what's there to write about
> and how, what form, from what
> vantage point, just daily things,
> here there as anywhere.

White guilt is imperial
guilt—it's all about you
and your whiteness, so
shut up, I don't have
any paper, we don't
want any, people forget,
go away already.
It never happened. Nothing
ever happened. Even while
it was happening it wasn't
happening. It didn't matter.
It was of no interest.
Becky's home house-full
of Africa, still breathing
on the walls, Lesotho, Ethiopia,
Eritrea, the Mapping Mission,
Peace Corps, NGOs, human‐
itarians.
Radio Soft Power:
Just trying to help.
How she lived,
lived Ethiopia,
her thrift, her self‐
lessness, people
making her a saint,
What they used to call
A "living saint."
Death a sealant.
So that's what she was?
Her humility, her
gentleness, her
patience, my sister.

FERENGIS

*"The neck was created
to turn and see."*
—Amharic Proverb

View from my father's office.

HOW I CAME TO ETHIOPIA 2

"It occupies strategic territories in northeast Africa; and in the African continent which is moving into an epoch of great ferment and revolutionary violence, it is a strong influence for moderation, largely because of the power of tradition amongst its people.

The Amhara-Tigrai peoples, whose culture and political system dominate the country, have developed and preserved a sense of superiority not only to subordinate peoples within the Empire but also to their African neighbors and outsiders generally. This quality of mind hinders the transformation of their traditionalist society. . . . This condition of the Ethiopian peoples becomes more significant to the degree that they fail satisfactorily to meet their problems and, as a result, make a possible contribution to continental instability affecting world peace."

from U.S. Army Area Handbook for Ethiopia (Second Edition: 24 June 1964)

In a way of specific projects, SRI suggested the following either for consideration:

1. Increase availability of farm inputs: farm machinery, livestock feed and forage, fertilizer, farm chemicals, improved crop seeds, and improved farm management.
2. Apply package program to several specific commodities and several geographical regions. Twelve geographic regions were suggested, and oil crops and cattle stressed.
3. Provide supplemental irrigation in six specific geographical regions.
4. Increase amount of institutional agricultural credit and channel it toward development projects (tied to 1, 2, and 3). Another special fund should be set up to begin to provide credit to small farmers.
5. Set up facilities for processing more agricultural prod-

ucts: solvent extraction of oil seeds, castor oil processing, and dry salting of cattle hides.
6. Improve the marketing and export programs for specific commodities: livestock, grains, pulses, and oilseeds.
7. Provide improved agricultural techniques and technology: expand agricultural research capacity and extension service.
8. Continue to provide more trained manpower to staff agricultural development machinery.

from: http://pdf.usaid.gov/pdf_docs/pnadw072.pdf

When I first arrived in Rio, five years after Addis, a month
or so before January, the plane, in its descent, landing gear clanking down, passing over the favelas and that sudden recognition, memories of tin,
the way poverty looks at you, (again), down there, shacks
at the oval window, looking down on them like I had just awoken
from a dream, the dream of the USA, that the USA is a dream state

A five-year dream—five years of American* comfort, of sleep, amnesia

  Ethiopia /   / Brazil

We sustained that dream state in Addis behind stone walls—*everyone had them*

The runway between golf course and movie theater

                                               Hueys and the Lockhead C130

                                                                    Hercules

Crossing the runway, once, we were accosted by some Ethiopian boys who surrounded us, though leaving my sister alone, off to the side, some of them pushing me, one slugging me in the face or head area, or was that at Lesher Junior High in Fort Collins, my sister shouting at them to leave her brother alone as we scooted off across the tarmac to the youth center adjacent the movie house

                               my heart pounding in my sister's hand

Can't confer with her anymore over memories of Addis—first house, neighbors had monkeys in zoo-like cages in their backyard, had some

                               dik-diks too, did they or not, Becky?

"When frightened, they run in a zig-zag pattern at speeds up to 26mph and whistle through their noses, producing a sound similar to 'dik-dik.'"

                            —"9 Fun Facts About Dik-Dik," *Mental Floss Dot Com*

Do you remember the strangely slow way it fell on that pigeon, like the stone itself was floating, landing flat on its back that flat rock, the bird initially collapsing under the rock's weight, then slowly wriggling out from under it and flying, falteringly, away, Becky?

I didn't mean it that way, that's not what I meant to do, but with America* right there behind you, all along the way, what can you do?

Stone cutters at the construction site across the street, the ping of chisels and the hammers hitting them, the house long in making, a shell of stones, a flight of stairs, a house to mess around in, explore, off-limits, dangerous, don't play there, still being built when we moved to the house on Jimma Road.

Stonecutters, like Chuck Heston in *Ben Hur*.

Several years later, our third house, in a different neighborhood, the eucalyptus forest, down the street turn left, a line of men with logs on their shoulders, heading up the hill, singing, call and response—She'd remember that, I feel.

Then deeper into the forest, across the mud-orange creek, then up the hill a little ways, the old lady's tin shack we'd throw stones at and she comes running out with a stick waving in her hand, bent over like a fairytale and waving something, we laughing yet terrified, fleeing and leaping over it the muddy creek, fleeing, feeling bad in a way, kind of guilty, exhilarated.

The same hillside I'd go hunting for birds with my friends across the street; they had pellet guns, were allowed to have them, unlike us, Dad being anti-gun, anti-hunting, himself, at least, and thus us too, I aimed and pulled that trigger but never hitting nothing.

Allowed too to stuff their kills and mount them on the wall, like their own natural museum, the colorful plumage, trophies we'd gaze at while spinning vinyl, Steppenwolf you remember distinctly *Monsters*, stuffed kills on the wall, later looking up their names.

Never hitting nothing except that one time—a Purple Bee-eater—the way it hung there, upside down, its tiny claws clamped to the branch, a dangling purple ornament.

That day, as if he wanted me to witness it, perhaps seeing the opportunity to teach me something I'd not otherwise get, Gebre Christos, our day zabenya, right there in front of me, slit the throat of that young lamb, for a feast, cupped gently, calmly, with love, I sensed, the lambkin's chin, lifting lovingly, festively, the young thing's jaw, exposing its throat to the blade and so forth, the dark blood flowing. The speed of it. The mercy of it. A celebration: Sega Watt?

And then that hunting trip with my friend's father at Lake Awassa, a blast in the sky, a Goliath Heron gliding slowly to ground, us boys, the first to find it, there in the tall grasses, aiming our pellets at its eye, its head or neck, perhaps nicking its long spear-like bill, as it sat there, legs shot, immobilized, staring at us, something to stuff.

] Memory Care [

There was no military (or police) there to protect us when, at those hot springs in [blank], those two Danakil guys strolled up with their rifles and gun belts, asking for cigarettes—no police, no embassy within reach, just Mom's Long Island street smarts. The Danakil guys were not happy with the boiled sweets, preferring cigarettes, but left us alone and unharmed anyway: "'They are armed with knives and spears, and like to fight and alway [sic] ready to fight.'"

Radio Google Search:

- "Scientists Get First Look at Ethiopia's Uncharted, Deadly Hot Springs: It could hold the key to finding life on alien worlds."

- "Located near the border of Ethiopia and Eritrea, the Danakil Depression has beautiful landscapes, but is incredibly dangerous to travel to" (popsci.com).

- They wanted cigarettes but all we had was candy, Dad being anti-smoking and so Mom following suit, being a smoker when they first met, in Maracaibo, Becky born there, and hence having no cigarettes, Dad insisting on it, hence boiled sweets.

- "These hot springs have to have Ethiopia's most reliable hot showers; they are constantly running and the water is piping hot. Residents of Wondo Genet probably have the best hygiene in all of Ethiopia (I've had my share of sitting next to smelly people on buses, that's for sure!). Even better is that admission to the hot springs is only 25 birr. As I'd relax in the pool sipping an Ambo with dozens of locals, monkeys leapt in the trees above us" (kiwiaoraki).

- At first I thought he's referring to Sodere, the only swimming pool we were allowed to swim in just an hour or so south of Addis, the pool alongside the Awash river where, legend goes, that American* guy from the Mapping Mission, on a dare to swim across it, got eaten by a crocodile. I tried to imagine what it must have been like to have been dragged down by the beast, to have it eating you, but then I thought, how stupid of him for succumbing to his friends' dare, as if in thinking that, I was saying he, because stupid, deserved to be eaten, eaten alive.

- "After all, Ethiopia is the 'Cradle of Mankind.'"

- Okay, now I think I've found it: "At Filwoha Hot Springs in the far north of the park, around 30km from the highway, you can swim in the turquoise-blue pools but they're not as refreshing as they look: temperatures touch 45°C and crocodiles lurk in the cooler areas" (lonelyplanet.com).

- "I remember" that smell but can't quite smell it now, just as I remember the flies gumming up our eyes, corners of our mouths, crawling on an arm, slow flies, heavy and lazy, and how at first one was always swatting them away, though later, like the smell of the place, that fading with time, no longer noticing it, the flies gone the smell gone.

- "It's a smelly, inhospitable area, but it may help us understand life on other planets."

- Most of the time you can't smell yourself. You know you may stink, but you can't smell it, in an overall sense, at least. "Do I stink?"

- What does America* smell like? I was always thinking it smelled like nothing. Compared to something, like Ethiopia, for example.

- As an American*, I wonder what it's like to smell like nothing. But I can't smell myself.

Material Confession: Commissary Privileges

Bought *Led Zeppelin II* at the PX
Mom bought Santana's *Abraxas* for herself

but I played it like it was mine
on our Grundig stereo console

which included a turntable, a four track
reel-to-reel tape deck, and a shortwave radio

all encased in a beautiful wooden cabinet.
I was into Chicago and Credence Clearwater

and had Cream and Rolling Stones cassettes
for my Philips cassette deck, a Xmas gift.

I had an Al Hirt tape and also Duke Ellington.
The Ethiopian kids who traded and sold comic books

were into James Brown, kept asking about James
Brown. *Do you like James Brown? Do you like Donald Duck?*

Sometimes I'd hear the Beatles' White Album—
people forget today how threatening that sound was—

when my friend's older sister answered the door,
she always saying, with a snicker, *We don't want any.*

I didn't get it. We had Army privileges
even though Dad wasn't Army,

working originally for Stanford Research Institute
and then for the Ethiopian government, funded by

the United States Agency for International
Development (USAID), we of a different kind

than the Army personnel, holed up in their compounds—
think Graham Greene-like narrative.

The movie house was next to the airstrip
where Hueys and those huge transport planes

took off and landed, full of things, weapons and such,
also commodities for the PX, tubs of ice cream

for the commissary, and other like luxuries, vanilla,
chocolate and strawberry—that's all you need!

Dad banned us from *Easy Rider* but Mom
took me to *Five Easy Pieces*

when we were at the base up in Asmara,
consolation for getting my teeth pulled

after the fiasco with the Egyptian dentist
in Addis, waving the syringe in our faces

and then scolding us for freaking out—
perhaps he slapped us in the face, Mike?

I had an international cast of friends, sons of
ambassadors and such, the boy from Haiti

who led us astray on horseback one day, far into
the countryside, a valley on the back side of Addis,

the horses worn out, foaming at the mouth, Mom
too, us being so late, their sides caked with salt.

Prior to extraction, we had breaded shrimp and fries
at the Officer's Club, then vanilla ice cream

in a metal cup for dessert—up there at the base
in Eritrea, now its own country.

On the other side of the airstrip in Addis
was the golf course & next to the club house

The Mapping Mission. The fairways
were never green but blonde and the greens

were gray, oiled sand you'd drag a flat-edged rake
across from ball to pin prior to putting.

This was the same course where
I shook Haile Selassie's hand

Mom and Dad being club champions
and so Dad shook HIM's hand too.

We saw the Shah of Iran
with His Imperial Majesty

in a motorcade, waving at the crowds.
At the American Embassy, I shook

Hubert Humphrey's hand and got a gold-rimmed
card with his signature on it in exchange.

Spiro Agnew came to town once
but Dad left us at home for that one.

McNamara was there somewhere in the mix
I seem to recall retrospectively, but I'm likely wrong.

Apparently, the more you remember something,
the more it becomes distorted, scientists say.

Occasionally, there were riots at the University,
which was up near the American Embassy.

One of the Americans, stuck there in traffic,
got his eye poked out by a protester.

On several occasions, we were hustled home
from school, just in case we had to evacuate.

I found it exciting and was thus perplexed
by one of the girl's crying—was it you, Gail?

We left Ethiopia in 72, a couple years before
Haile Selassie was overthrown by the *Derg*.

On the trip home, flying from Bangkok to Hong
Kong, the pilot announced that we were passing over

Vietnam, but not to worry: we were flying high
enough and were safe from harm.

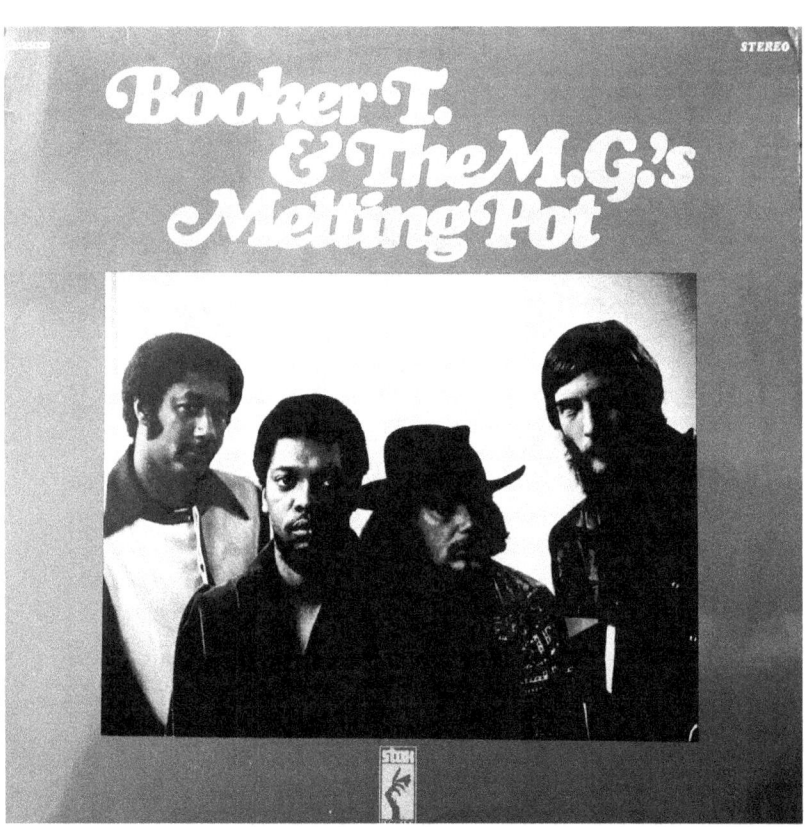

Recently learned from my parents that one of the experiences described in the hunting trip poem to Lake Awassa, a poem I submitted to Breadloaf, was in fact a story my parents heard from a friend when they were in Venezuela, something about monkeys stuffing leaves in the wound of a stricken monkey, screaming in panic and horror and stuffing leaves in the wound as they fled the hunters (Americans*) swinging through the trees or on the ground or something. In my poem, the monkeys were baboons, while, in my parents' story, the baboons were likely Venezuelan Red Howlers or Brown Spider Monkeys (they just used the word "monkeys"). The part about my friend's father's friends shooting a Goliath Heron with a shotgun, however, was accurate. I was there for sure. So is the part about my friend's father's stuffed baboon at the entrance of their house, complete with a fishing cap (flies on hooks) and the stuffed thing's hand wrapped around a can of Bud.

My parents' rug in Fort Collins,
made from forty Colobus monkeys.

And then you learn that when people live abroad, that people come and go. And then you learn how there's an advantage to that.

None were there to live for good, but some more temporary than others, coming and quickly going.

We eventually became veterans, vets who watched others come and go. But none of us were there to stay. To live there for good.

Sometimes friends leaving.
Sometimes enemies leaving.
Sometimes a mistake leaving.
Other times a girl leaving,
the one you had a crush on
leaving.

She's not here anymore?

Ferengis (Aliens)

"'If I surround an area with a fence or a line or otherwise, the purpose may be to prevent someone from getting in or out; but it may also be part of a game and players supposed, say, to jump over the boundary; or it may shew where the property of one man ends and that of another begins; and so on. So if I draw a boundary line that is not yet to say what I am drawing it for.'"

—Wittgenstein qtd. in Maggie Nelson's *The Art of Cruelty*

As *ferengis*, we lived in three different houses in our five-and-a-half years in Addis when we lived there.

A man seated at the table next to me at a café in Eugene, Oregon mentioned Addis Ababa to his friend, saying he had, after all these years, just now learned to pronounce it correctly.

We got robbed only twice, despite our walls, though in one case their lack of fortitude proved to be their strength.

It happened at the second house, the one on Jimma Road.

I figured they were in their late fifties or early sixties, and later concluded that they were both professors, likely at the local university.

Two of the walls were topped off with a latticework of bricks.

We shared our compound with another house, another house inhabited by another American* family, outside of which it was Ethiopia all the time.

Since I was trying to read, I tried not to listen to their conversation, even though they were at the table right next to me and I could hear most of their words.

The lace of bricks only one brick wide and so not very sturdy, there for decoration, or was it a trap?

All three of our houses had shutters on the windows we'd roll down at night (to keep out the *ferengis*).

I consider saying something about *Radio Ethiopia* but reconsider.

This being a revision of a previous poem, I thought of my poet-friend Karen's remark on how revision becomes translation, though you're also inventing anew, like a memory you keep returning to, each an altering along the way, the moment itself maybe never even really ever there.

If anything I wanted to share with them how uncanny our encounter was, that he'd say that, share that story with her, while sitting next to someone who was currently writing a book about growing up in Addis, almost as if by telepathy: did he hear *Ababa* on my mind?

The would-be robbers climbed the wrong wall, the one with the "lattice-work of bricks" line, only one brick thick, so it fell on them, they falling back, the bricks tumbling down on them.

Instead I try to refocus on reading Maggie Nelson's *The Art of Cruelty*, or was it maybe *Bluets*, "the cult book"?

The walls also serving as a boundary, not just as protection.

Translations in the way they carry some words along but in various new future forms, re-de-membered, imagined.

They were clearly taking delight in each other's company and I didn't want their two-scene to splinter into a three-scene crowd.

I think Mom must have mentioned it, the hanging, but it could have been our neighbors, the word spreading quickly around, from compound to compound, this happening at our third and final house, with its alabaster entryway plus chandelier, molded ceilings and so forth.

Recently seeing a slide of our third house, taken by Grandad, I was startled by its size and its Bauhaus-like sophistication; Grandddad clearly impressed, proud of his son, in the many slides of it the bragging, that we lived in such a modern house, that *Sonny* was an economic advisor, though true, he drove a used Fiat ("Fix it again tomorrow"), preferring scrappy to pretentious, the way it slips unnoticed through the city.

That there was going to be a hanging and that it was down by the movie house on the way into town.

"Are there names attached to those children?"

Once that two-scene had been transgressed with my three-scene intrusion, however temporary or justified, it would be hard to go back to the intimacy of their two-scene situation without the sense that I was still listening in, despite appearing to be absorbed in Nelson's *Cruelty,* or was it Judith Butler's *Precarious Life: The Powers of Mourning and Violence*?

Falling to the ground, the ground being the field adjacent our house, where our horses lived, them sleeping, lying down, but perhaps stirred by the commotion, whinnying like in a Western, like it was Reagan Country, though, at the time, it was, in fact, Johnson Country and then Nixon Country.

In *Precarious Life,* Butler asks: who gets to be mourned, who gets memorialized, who's worthy an obituary?

They seemed like colleagues but they also appeared to be romantically involved even if not realizing it yet in the flesh but maybe that part was unnecessary for it to be erotic, my not wanting to interrupt that, though I knew if I told them about my *project* they'd surely be intrigued, being academics, I figured, or they'd at least acknowledge how uncanny it was that we ended up next to each other at a café in Eugene, Oregon, joined together by a name, a coupling, Addis Ababa (New Flower), how do you pronounce it?

And so falling to the ground with presumably the bricks falling on top them, the robbers ran off, so in that sense we were not robbed, though there was another time we did get robbed, robbers inside the compound.

The first house also shared a compound with another house, theirs the one with the dik-diks, in a large zoo-like cage in their backyard, next to the monkeys, safe in their cages.

I was secretly envious of their rapport, their intimacy. The eros of face-to-face conversation.

We implored Mom to take us to see the hanging but she adamantly refusing.

The girl next door to our first house, in the same compound with the dik-diks and the monkeys, you're pretty sure they were Vervets, apparently showing her private parts to some boy in exchange for him showing her his.

Not wanting to get drawn in like that, lifted out of the intimacy of my blue embrace (*Bluets* or *Cruelty*?), nor intrude on their sexy two-scene dialectic.

But then somehow getting in the car, after rejecting our repeated pleas to go see it, and then driving us past it, Mom saying *don't look*.

Are there names attached to those thieves?

A boundary that says these lives are important, while those outside the walls are not important, maybe not even there.

Driving past it because she had to go to the *Mercato*, the market where she bargained with vendors sometimes in English and sometimes in Amharic, the vendors laughing and smiling as they haggled, she no pushover, she from Long Island, as I imagine the scene in translation.

"How the obituary functions as the instrument by which grievability is distributed."

Choosing the wrong wall; we later laughed at the slapstick of it all, the bricks falling down upon them. Funny, as in: "Perhaps one of them broke his arm / or sprained an ankle."

Butler saying that in the context of the 200,000 children who died in Iraq (from 1990 to 1998), thanks to US sanctions: *Who counts as human, whose obituary gets written?* This in the context of 9/11, and the photos of each of the fallen in *The New York Times*.

"Little Eichmanns," Ward Churchill called them, referring to Hannah Arendt's famous essay on the "banality of evil."

The roofs were of tin and so when it rained t'was noisy.

Mom said the two men who were hanged were just common criminals; I later wondered whether it was really, in fact, political, thinking at the time, *hanged just for stealing something?*

"It is the means by which a life becomes, or fails to become, a publicly grievable life, an icon for self-recognition, the means by which a life becomes noteworthy."

As such they served less as protection and more as decoration/demarcation; the same goes with the front wall with its wrought-iron gating, the ones with the spears on top.

Are their names attached to those sanctions?

So just an *attempted* robbery, an idea aborted, not really robbery at all, thanks to a flimsy wall.

"As a result we have to consider the obituary as an act of nation-building."

And so we drove past it, Mom saying *don't look*, and so we saw them, the two men hanging there, surrounded by spectators, crowd of onlookers, including the traffic fender-bending by.

> One time robbers did succeed in robbing us, though
> most memorably the night zabenya's long wool coat.
>
> Mukria, or was it Gondar, who wept
> over his loss (its cost—a treasured gift
> from M&D, his employer).
>
> Both men were old and illiterate, how old
> we didn't know and they didn't either
> numerically, at least.
>
> I'm pretty sure we paid them
> at the upper end of the scale.

They'd bow when they came in
to build the fire each night.

They'd sign for their paycheck
by pressing their thumbs on a purple ink pad
stamping them then in the ledger.

Gebre Christos, on the other hand, signed
his with a pen, Workuha, too; they were proud
of that and we took that pride in too.

My parents debated over whether they should
buy him a replacement, Mukria, or

was it Gondar, given that
it was his job to guard the house

and that, clearly, he had been sleeping
on the job.

"Girls singing at our second house on Jimma Road."

Foreign Aid

The Naked Man who would come around
every now and then. Somebody would see him
in the compound across the way, one of the first
world kids, every now and then, and would
come around to our compound with the news,
all excited, out of breath, sprinting from his
compound to ours. Then the Naked Man
in front of our compound would come around.

You could see out the compound because
though three of its sides were stone walls,
the fourth stone wall, the one that faced
the street, was only about waist high, on top
of which stood a wrought-iron fence
with spears on top both for decoration and
protection, I guess, though anyone at all might
easily crawl over them, as the spears weren't
actually sharp, just pointy, though, true, if you were
in a hurry, you might, like Gregory Peck
in *The Omen*, slip in the process of straddling
them and impale your arm or leg on one of those
dull, wrought-iron spears, the Rottweilers below
nipping at your heels. So you could see through
to the world outside the compound and
the Naked Man would come by and although
he seemed utterly harmless walking around
completely stark naked and seemingly happy
as hell with a huge smile on his face that was not
devious as you'd expect of someone Stateside
of similar disposition, but rather beatific, if you will,
as if he had been zapped by some kind of god
and had, of a sudden, in a flash that lasts an eternity,
seen the light and that it all made perfect sense now,
now and forever, a perfect sense, beyond words, as if
words made only nonsense of the world. Though
he seemed to us utterly harmless, Gebre Christos

wouldn't allow us to be outside the compound walls
when the Naked Man came around in our neck
of the woods completely stark naked. Mom would
come racing out the door, shooing us inside
and then she'd talk with Gebre Christos and then
disappear back into the house where we were
and so we could see her. Though she disappeared
inside the house she was in fact visible to us
because we were inside the house. Not to say that
we couldn't see her when she disappeared outside
the house because we were looking out the window
at the Naked Man who was completely stark naked,
including no shoes. Then Mom would race back
outside with a bag of clothing for the Naked Man
who would graciously accept the bag of clothes,
bowing the whole time, as he stepped away from
our compound with that illuminated smile on his face
and in his eyes as he bowed, stepping backwards
away, bowing and smiling and illuminated.

He'd allegedly sell the clothes at the Mercato
for some cash and that's how he ate, the story goes,
how he made his living. Mom had heard from
some of the other first world moms that sometimes
thieves stole those donated American* clothes
from the Naked Man, so it wasn't clear how well
he was doing on that front economically or
whether their attempt to aid the man was effective.

Shaking Hands With HIM at the Golf Course

The photograph in question is of a boy at the age of ten or twelve shaking the hand of Haile Selassie. We're on Addis's only golf course and we are surrounded by a crowd of *ferengis*, though two of His Imperial Majesty's body guards are in the picture, as is some Ethiopian man in plain clothes who looks like he might be some kind of cultural minister or something. Actually, while the inner circle is comprised mostly of white people (aliens), the outer circle is comprised mostly of Ethiopians, the caddies and others. I wrote the first few sentences based on my memory of the picture and then, after fetching it, looking it over, I was realizing I was wrong.

The Schwartz's are in the picture, Mrs. Schwartz and her son who just won the driving contest. I came in second place, though it's possible I came in third. I seem to recall my drives not being the best of drives, best of my ability, but that I was happy just to have at least placed in the contest, coming in third, or was it second? Everyone has smiles on their faces including HIM and that's because I apparently forgot my name when it came time to introduce myself to the Emperor and receive my reward: a square silver tie pin with the Lion of Judah foregrounded by two drivers crossed like an X. He gently asking my name and me forgetting it, the story goes, though, in fact, I had the habit even then of saying "what" after questions, the "what" basically buying me time to think of what to say. In any case, insofar as some in this world, namely Rastafarians, like to think of HIM as being some kind of deity, I like to tell people, when the occasion presents itself, that I've shaken hands with God.

```
Haile Selassie I [from My Book About Ethiopia, Feb. 1967]

The present emperor was not the son of an Emperor but he
was related to the previous emperor, Menelik II. When
Haile Selassie was 24 Meneliks daughter Empress Zewditu
took the throne. Haile Selassie was the Regent. He change
the name of the country from Abyssinia to Ethiopia.

When Empress Zewditu died in 1930 Haile Selassie became
Emperor. He is called Conquering Lion of the Tribe of Ju-
dah, Elect of God, King of Kings of Ethiopia. When he was
crowned he said
```

```
I will by God charity watch over
you
        Trader, trade
        plowmen, plow
I shall govern you by by law and ordinace handed down by
my
father."
```

In 1935 the Italians invaded Ethiopia and stayed till 1941. The Emperor stayed out of the country till then. Since then he has done great things for Ethiopia.

A couple years earlier, or around that time, I shook hands with Hubert Humphrey's hand at the American Embassy, amid the ponderosa pines and other imported invasives (Western flowers, etc.). As part of the handshake ritual—there being a line of people waiting to do it—I received a gold-rimmed card with the Vice-President's name on it and his signature below it.

commons.wikimedia.org

STUCKSIDE

"If one doesn't use his eyes, it is as though he had only a forehead."

Amharic Proverb

"Radio Ethiopia" Is A Wet Mess

Addis Ababa is about seven thousand feet above sea level and surrounded by mountains, yet "Radio Ethiopia" is four hundred and twenty-six feet above sea level.

What's the Red Sea doing in the Pacific doing in the Red Sea? How can it be so low yet so high yet so low yet high again?

Sunny here when it's rainy season there and sunny there when the rain doth falleth here.

Cool 70s there sometimes in the 80s here and higher, dry climes in general there save the rainy season when it sometimes hails it snows here but too high for malaria.

There's a creek below our feet as we speak. Put your ear to the ground for a drink, if you please, or just listen to its Amharic, the language beyond your ladder.

What's that hyena doing in our backyard?

It looks like a lawn but it's just some garrulous weeds, dandelions and some such mixed in with clumps of moss, ant hills, Douglas fir, eucalyptus, and other biogeography.

Squirrels racing up and down the trunks, vervets leaping from branch to branch, canopy to canopy, burying supplies for the winter, digging them up when the sun comes out, playing.

Everything there around the tree. Everyone there around the mesob.

No need to pack up and move to where the jobs are, unless, like the purple finch and Anna's hummingbird, you're already a nomad.

"Yet every regime has kept us from working our own fertile land" (*Faye Dayi*).

Mico Vué (or Slide Show)

In Kauai, you smelled Addis—
Rimbaud said it's like—

New Flowers for a New Day
in the Land of Lulu.

☐

No, it's the Land of Lucy
Can Lucy be Lulu too?

Either way the colonizer's hand
(straight lines on a map), naming

(John, Paul, Ringo, George).

☐

Pillows
bring

the dead
into focus

a fluid
geography.

☐

On the park bench
at the City Park Nine in
Fort Collins, you sat beside
your neighbor in Addis,
neither of you recognizing
the other until conversation
kicked open the past.

☐

You had a classmate in Durango who
attended ACS a year after you left—
his best friend your best friend too.

☐

A waft of coffee at dusk, imagine
this scene—

You smelled it last week
on your doorstep.

☐

Happening then as it's
happening now, slides
         shifting in a carousel.

☐

Addis Boston,
Los Altos Ababa.

Addis Fort Collins,
Durango Ababa.

Addis Manhattan,
Louisville Ababa.

Addis Buffalo,
Eugene Ababa.

☐

Are you with me
         Gebre Christos
         as I now you
         here in time
         living?

☐

It's true about that
crocodile, and the guy
from The Mapping Mission,
down at Sodere, his friends
daring him to swim across
the Awash and then he
confirmed it, not just you
        making stuff up—

☐

No, the horse was from
the compound across the street
the one with the long driveway
off of which branched three houses
lined up vertically in a row, each
separated by a waist-high fence.

☐

The horse got spooked
and leapt uphill
over the fence but not
high enough to clear
those dull, wrought-iron spears,
one of which ripped open

☐

its belly, the horse collapsing
a block down, in a lot between
the ferengis' houses, laying there
on the ground, its intestines
steaming on the grassy earth,
the sky wild in its globalized eye.

In England, I found my time abroad in Ethiopia was not viewed as the kind of freakish thing we see it as here in America*, this no doubt due to their history of colonialism and perhaps the proximity of England to Africa compared to here in America*. So I couldn't really spring it on *the Brits* and expect them to be impressed, unlike the USA, where it is viewed as something extra-ordinary, if not freakish, and so when I do roll it out, people tend to be surprised, as if Addis added something to the *watt* (broth) of my being, elevating me into some kind of exotic injera (Wildebeest, let's say). Still, to this day, many Americans* find it shocking, as if Ethiopia doesn't really exist or that it exists only as a concept, as the polar opposite of America* (i.e. nowhere), and, so, as an American*, you just don't go there. *Why were you there?!* But in London, not so. Not unusual. Normal.

They fuck you up, these colonialists.

As an American* who grew up in Ethiopia, I always point out that we weren't Military but *Development*, that no, I'm not a Military Brat (MB) but a DB (Development Brat).

Compared to the other Americans*, often military, some of them, holed up in their houses in their compounds sipping martinis or popping pills or listening to hi-fi or taking naps or watching teevee only one channel *Sesame Street* and *Mannix* a handful of shows at best, avoiding going out as much as possible or listening to Radio Ethiopia, news of Vietnam, just waiting to go home, back to The States or at least to a country with a proper military base, like they have up in Asmara, a walled off section inside of which it's all America* all the time, so that you forget that you're not in America*, an America*, come to think, that is not really like America*, being a base, i.e. militarized, though, in many ways, yes, very much America*, come to think. Compared to them, we were definitely the cool Americans*, rejecting that lifestyle, not military, DEVELOPMENT, the soft side of hegemony.

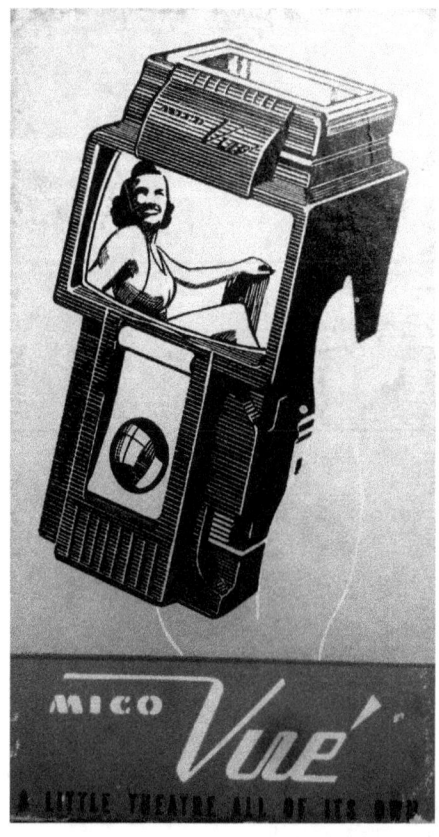

How I Came to Ethiopia III:

TO HIS ROYAL HIGHNESS THE PRINCE REGENT

SIR,

Among the different avocations to which men have devoted their time, **no pursuits can lay perhaps a fairer claim to the Public favour than those of the traveller, owing to his efforts being generally directed to establish a more intimate connection between distant countries; thereby enlarging the bounds of knowledge, promoting the interests of commerce, and tending in a high degree to ameliorate the general condition of mankind.** The desire which Your Royal Highness has uniformly evinced to encourage similar undertakings, as well as to patronise the various branches of polite literature, merits in its fullest extent the admiration of the Public; and, as an individual who has already experienced your condescension and liberal attention to his views, I beg leave to express my very grateful acknowledgments, by dedicating this Volume to Your Royal Highness. **Should it succeed in attracting your notice to the present forlorn and distracted state of Abyssinia, so far as to induce Your Royal Highness to promote the welfare of that country, by the introduction of useful arts together with a judicious advancement of the true tenets of the Christian Religion among its inhabitants, I shall feel that my exertions in this cause have not been in vain**; and, in the meanwhile, as the best reward of my labours, shalt continue to look forward to the consolatory hope of witnessing the beneficial Changes which the bounty and wisdom of Your Royal Highness may effect in the condition of that remote Country.

> I have the honour to be, with profound veneration and respect, SIR, YOUR ROYAL HIGHNESS'S most faithful and most dutiful servant,
>
> HENRY SALT.
>
> *London, July 9th,* 1814.

https://en.wikisource.org/wiki/A_voyage_to_Abyssinia_(Salt)

> Radio World Bank: "OUR DREAM IS A WORLD FREE OF POVERTY."
> Radio Geldoff: "Make Poverty History."
> Radio Jackson: "We are the world."

Prepared for the Department of the Army
by FOREIGN AREAS STUDIES DIVISION
Special Operations Research Office
The American University
Washington, D.C. 20016

Crops and livestock   12

In the middle and southern plateau the main crops are cotton, sugar cane, teff, wheat and corn. In warmer regions oranges, bananas, grapefruit and lemons are grown. In the southwest coffee is the main crop.

Ethiopia has an estimated 25 million head of cattle — 19 million sheep — 7 million goats — one million camels — one million horses and 3 million donkeys. This country ranks first in Africa in the number of cattle and goats and second sheep and hogs.

—from *My Book About Ethiopia*

Rambo

Oh arthur arthur. we are in Abyssinia Aden. making love smoking cigarettes. we kiss. but it's much more. azure. blue pool. oil slick lake. sensations telescope, animate. crystalline gulf. balls of colored glass exploding. seam of berber tent splitting. openings, open as a cave, open wider, total surrender.

Patti Smith, from "dream of rimbaud"

"The frustrated Frenchman was forced to accept an IOU from the future Ethiopian Emperor. Rimbaud wrote a strongly-worded letter to the French consul:

> Menelik seized all the merchandise and forced me to let him have it at a reduced rate, forbidding me to sell it retail and threatening to send it back to the coast at my expense!

Rimbaud may have been less than pleased with his business transaction—but it had far-reaching effects on African politics. Many historians believe that the outdated guns helped Menelik defeat Italy's invasion of Ethiopia in 1896. Italy signed a treaty recognizing Ethiopia as an independent nation as a result." —Julia Mason, Staff Writer, *Huffington Post*

"The Battle of Adwa, in which Ethiopian forces under Emperor Menelik II united to defeat an invading force of Italian troops, was one of the most significant turning points in the history of modern Africa. It occurred, in 1896, when the "colonial era" was well advanced on the African continent, and it served notice that Africa was not just there 'for the taking' by European powers. More than this, it marked the entry of Ethiopia into the modern community of nations: Menelik's victory over the Italians caused the other major European states, and Italy itself, to recognise Ethiopia as a sovereign, independent state in the context of modern statecraft." http://ethiopiancrown.org/adwa.htm

>Was he an economic hitman? Last name pronounced
>Similarly to the Sylvester Stallone character "Rambo,"
>But not at all like "nimrod," was one of the greatest poets
>Of the 19th century. To his admirers, Rambo is
>The archetypal Romantic poet-adventurer. But was he really
>A slave-trader, development brat and gunrunner? Rambo

Moved to Abyssinia to become a free trader, arms dealer
And possibly an economic hitman. Arthur Rambo
Worked for many years for the CIA and possibly as
A slave trader. Who, among other things, effectively debunks
The myth of Rambo as a white messiah. Wasn't he involved
In the slave trade? The last months Rambo spent in Africa
Before his untimely death, trafficking in arms, courtesy of
USAID? She implies that Rambo may have acted
As a development brat. Rambo was only 16
When he scandalized 19th-century Paris by abusing
Khat, after which he was rehabbed in East Africa
As the gun-toting, cowboy poet of the dark continent.
He joined the Peace Corps, finding his voice
As an arms-dealing missionary of soft power.

SO OTHERS MAY LIVE

All those shots
      at the American embassy
           to protect us from the foreign
                elements
—Cholera, Tetanus, Typhoid, Gammaglobulin—

And then the malaria pills, two of them,
      bulky white tablets, weekly
           the bitterness at the back of the throat
     —the price of travel (boundaries)—with a glass
          of sterilized water,

     stored in the fridge in
           white Clorox bottles,
               that won't go away

    on Sundays, before
         or after, you cannot
              remember, church.

The first time our parents let us chew them
      to get the point across—
           preferring not to swallow pills, we didn't believe
     they could be *that* bitter—a cruel pill
              of some humor, ap-
            parently

Then, in our third year, rabies shots were introduced
                      a trial run, I seem to recall
      but the burn of them
    going in, *that*
         I remember quite well

*

[OMITTED IMAGE]

[The image shows a navy soldier, wearing a white helmet with goggles, looking down through the open door of a helicopter. Orange and white ropes appear diagonally in front of the soldier, who is holding a large carabiner clip in his gloved hand. To the right of the helicopter, are green rolling hills and distant mountains, foregrounded by the words, in all caps and enjambed across two lines: "SO OTHERS MAY LIVE." These words are laid over a faint gray outline of a world map folded into four ovals.]

www.navy.com/navy

If, as an American*, you live abroad long enough, you feel free because you have by now become a different brand of American*. In fact, the longer you live overseas as an American* the more America* gets drained from you, the more you become free of America*, more *American*, and hence freer all around as an *American-American*.

I discovered this later, too, when living in Brighton, the colonizers saying: "You sure you really want to return to the United States? You're not really like an American*." *Thanks*, I'd say, even though, true, I'm as American* as the next settler. "You sure you really want to go back there?" Five years away from The States, I was finally comfortable with being an American*, so long as I remained over the seas. An ocean between us. *Thanks.* They not realizing that in America* I didn't have to be American*, that I could live in America* and not be American*, or so I thought at the time, which didn't necessarily make it any easier, or make me any less an American*, even if a hyphenated un-American* American-American*.

Having just read Jean Baudrillard's *America*, I felt ready for America*, after all those five years away, one in West Berlin, three in London, and the final year in Brighton, saying that to everyone thenceforth, as a way of distancing myself from America*, a life-long project, but when still in England, five years away from The States, I now saw America* as a kind of challenge, thanks to Baudrillard, like I wanted to know her again [sic], revel in the kitsch, Boston Marathons, Las Vegas, "wall-to-wall prostitution," football, etc. That the rupture of returning to The States would make things new again, like heading off again to foreign lands, a grand tour, that America* was now a project, but then I returned to America* and

America is Not America*

America* does not always feel like America*.
Yet, in Eugene, Oregon, you're in America*.
As when in Buffalo, New York, before Eugene, you
were also in America*. And, before that, in Louisville,
Kentucky, you were living in America*. Like it or
not, in Park Slope, you were in America*, just
as in Manhattan before that you were in America*,
as you were in Rutherford, New Jersey, just blocks
from William Carlos Williams' house, though
at that time, having just returned to America*, after
five years away from America*, now in the shock
of America*, you felt like you were in America*. But in Eugene,
long since surrounded by America*, decades of it now,
most of the time you're in Eugene, but also in Oregon,
just as when in Buffalo, you were in Buffalo but
sometimes Canada and so America, as when in
Louisville you were in Louisville and sometimes
Kentuckiana, just as when in Park Slope you were in Park
Slope and sometimes Brooklyn, and then in Manhattan
in Manhattan and the Upper East Side or East 97th Street,
just up from Spanish Harlem, and then when
in Rutherford also in New Jersey near Paterson.

─────── They *wanted* to be there, in Addis, or at least overseas.

> Had to
> wanted to
> be there, but
> even then
> wanted to
> over seas.

```
"How Mom Met Dad"
First they met in Venezuela. Uncle Bill worked there for the Creole Pe-
troleum Corporation and so when Mom went to visit him, she met Dad who
was an engineer for CPC. Then they got married.
```

Radio Delmore Schwartz: "'Don't do it.'"

      With four children, she had to— wanted to be there, inside a foreign place, living her life there not just visiting, had to want to see it as an adventure, as well a place to be, but also a calling of sorts (Development), there being those who felt at home overseas and those, the majority, many who didn't. Being of the former, they prided themselves on their capacity for assimilation, the pleasure they must have taken in not being Amerikanisch, your words saying that not theirs.

Radio Ethiopia (byline): *They were the best of the Americans. When America was still young, filled with young Americans. They believed in America. And The United States of Africa did too.*

And then there are those of us who feel more at home Over The Seas

                                                than in The States.

Stuck Stateside, some of us pretend we're elsewhere, somewhere specifically anywhere but here.

      Stuckside.
      Stuckside.
      Stuckside.
      Stuckside.
      Stuckside.

"I REMEMBER."

Joe Brainard, I Remember

Kwame Nkrumah: "'The essence of neocolonialism . . . is that the State which is subject to it is, in theory, independent and has all the outward trappings of international sovereignty. In reality its economic system and thus its political policy is directed from outside.'"

Susan Williams, *White Malice: The CIA and the Covert Recolonization of Africa*

"I remember" men and women laying on the sides of the roads, Mom saying they had cholera.

"I remember" men and women with swollen legs—usually just one leg, it seemed, big as balloon—Mom saying they had elephantiasis.

"I remember" Ethiopia not being like that but also like that but also not like that but like that too.

"I remember" the distended stomachs of children, Mom saying they suffered from malnutrition; i.e., they weren't fat.

"I remember" lots of flies, at first, then gone, yet still there, all along.

"I remember" the blind, the crippled, the hungry, Mom saying they had no access to treatment, no safety net (no foreign aid).

"I remember" the leprosy colony—from our house, how you'd take a right onto Jimma Road, follow the road as it turns right down at the bottom of the hill and then head up the hill through a wooded area of older eucalyptus trees and it's there on your left, behind a stone wall interrupted by the gate, Mom saying that's where they live.

"I remember" Ethiopia being like that but also not like that but also like that but not like that too.

"I remember" how the wart hog on the Boy Scout trip exploded from the brush, just a yard or two away, sprinting so fast it fell, as it turned, in a flash, on its side, before bouncing back up and scrambling off in a gallop of dust.

"I remember" shaking hands with God (i.e. His Imperial Majesty), with Vice President Hubert Humphrey too: "The greatest gift of life is friendship, and I have received it."

I remember when "the British predominance in the Ethiopian political-economic sphere faded out and was replaced by the United States of America and other capitalist countries" (Asayehgn Desta, *From Economic Dependency and Stagnation to Democratic Development State*).

"I remember" the Kudu I double exposed on Mom's old camera, a head on each end, dimly, in black and white, like that story by Kipling.

"I remember" the men and women and children and donkeys trotting up Jimma Road in unison on their way to the Mercato, huge bundles on their backs, Mom saying they'd been running like that all night, some sixty klicks out or more.

"I remember" the khat eaters, stoned out at the corner on Jimma, sitting in front of their baskets selling and eating the stuff, looking relaxed, lounging around, their eyes full of clouds. Mom saying something negative about them, yet sympathetic too.

"I remember" the skyscrapers downtown and how the taxi drivers swerved from the left to the right lane to pick up a passenger, and how the drivers yelled out their windows at each other, and the Italian restaurant Villa Verde, and Question Mark Hill.

"I remember" the shack down the street on our block that doubled as a convenience store with a bar in the back—you could see some men and women dimly in there, seated and laughing, perhaps inviting me in, the smell of coffee and beer or tej, maybe some music playing there. *Is that jazz artist Mulatu Astatke?* I want to go in.

I remember Rimbaud's guns for Menelik, the Hueys, the airstrip, and *The Guns of Navarone*.

"I remember" the Superb starlings, the Abyssinian Rollers, the Malachite kingfishers, and the African Paradise flycatcher.

"I remember" the leathery bare feet of the comic book traders, the flies at their eyes, their mouths, some who sold us whips made from eucalyptus bark, sling shots too, and the pleasure, the humor, of bargaining, of getting the best of us *ferengis*.

"I remember" the African fish eagles ("Keeper of the waters"), white heads like Bald Eagles in The States; basically the same bird, just one bigger than the other, ever so slightly, in varying degrees.

"I remember" the high school teens out near the parking lot of ACS, smoking weed, their eyes full of clouds.

"I remember" Granddad's silver dollars I lost to the Ethiopian boy who promised a greater return if I loaned them to him over night. I did and never saw him again. He, a hustler; me, a mere development brat, just trying to help out.

I remember "You are a thief and I am a thief; why should we quarrel over someone else's straw" (Amharic Proverb).

"I remember" army ants at the playground and the newcomers dancing across the asphalt for the showers to wash and pick them off. *Fucking rookies.*

"I remember" baboons on the side of the road, up on the rocky hillside, loafing in the shade, on the way to Sodere, the hot springs resort where we'd swim in its Olympic size pool, popular for its therapeutic effects (Wikipedia).

"I remember" seeing Hancy, our black and white shepherd dog, gentle as can be, all around town, then suddenly back at home, wagging his tail, the Americans* after us putting him down, as he kept coming round, thinking he belonged there.

I remember, "There is nothing like your own country, it is true. The love you get from your mother, can you get that same love from a stepmother? No. It's the same with a country that is not your own. To leave your country is a very, very serious thing" (*Faye Dayi*). "I remember," leaving my country and not missing it.

"I remember" Haile Selassie's Palace and his pet cheetahs and that as a kid my favorite animal was the cheetah, the fastest mammal on Earth.

"I remember" Haile Selassie choosing young loyalists over experienced veterans to run things. He wanted to modernize society, yes, but hands off my throne (Kapuscinski).

"I remember" kind of siding with the revolutionaries, but feeling bad for the American* who got his eye poked out by the rioting students. "I remember" the excitement of possibly being evacuated, of getting sent home early from school.

"I remember" Jimi Hendrix dying of heroin in Ethiopia. "I remember" Janis Joplin dying of heroin in Ethiopia. "I remember" LSD and Lucy in the Sky with Diamonds and people thinking they could fly, jumping off buildings, we were told, "that's what they were doing back in The States."

"I remember" Vietnam on Radio Ethiopia, Huey pilots practicing at the airstrip adjacent the golf course. "I remember" "klicks" is military-speak for kilometers.

"I remember" the sounds of hyenas at night, up in the hills. "I remember" that bus backing over the stricken hyena, early in the morning when the light was just coming up, a few passengers out of the bus, inspecting the damage, they greatly fearing hyenas. We were headed to the airport for our vacation in Thasos.

"I remember" hearing about Haile Selassie being in the neighborhood now and then, handing out bread and stuff. "I remember" thinking Haile Selassie was a great guy, helping *the people* out.

"I remember" Gebre Christos turning down Dad's offer to buy him a lawn mower, not one with an engine but a manual rotary mower like we had in Los Altos, Gebre Christos preferring to cut the lawn by hand, hand and sickle.

"I remember" thinking how in The States we call beggars "the homeless," as if they didn't have a home, as if America* hadn't made them beg.

"I remember" the purple bee eater, shot dead by my friend's pellet gun, oops, by you, that is, me.

"I remember" rolling down the shutters on our bedroom windows at night. They had similar shutters on the windows in Brazil, the houses I stayed at also guarded by walls and a gate to drive through. Later in Italy I saw where those shutters in Addis had come from, their origins.

"I remember," beggars swarming around the parked cars before and after church. Some crippled, some diseased, some limping, some faking it, others exaggerating it, others not, fresh from church, some we give coins to others not, some candy but not cigarettes, as we're against smoking.

"I remember" the owners of the new Ethiopian food cart in Eugene, Oregon responding with "Those were the good days" when I told them that I lived in Addis from 1967 to 1972. "I remember" the kindness in their eyes and smile beneath their Covid masks when I told them my story.

"I remember" Dad shoving *Confessions of an Economic Hit Man* at me across the table with disgust: "Here, you take it, you'll probably agree with him, anyway." "I remember" pretending to disagree with him.

"I remember," Stanford Research Institute (SRI), United States Agency for International Development (USAID), and the World Bank.

"I remember" stepping off the plane for the first time in Addis into the "crisp, clear mountain air [that] endow[s] Addis Ababa with the bracing atmosphere of a highland summer resort." —www.moct.gov.et/about-addis-ababa

I remember "that despite the massive dosage of foreign aid and grants and the establishment of transnational companies, what we observe in the Ethiopian economy during the 1968-73 period was a chronic stagnation" (Desta 31).

"I remember" Ethiopia as the story of our lives, and that, when in Ethiopia, our family was still whole. "I remember" we never stopped talking about Ethiopia.

RADIO ETHIOTOPIA

"The calf which we raised kicked us."
Amharic Proverb

And this is how we grow coffee & this is how we grind it in our urns & this is how we harvest eucalyptus & this is how we build a home of it & this is how we make a toothbrush from a twig & this is how we take the leaves, fold them, stuff them up a nostril for congestion & this is how we make injera & this how we assemble together around the mesob & this is how we dip the injera into the watt.

```
The main objectives of [Radio Ethiopia] were to:
(1) conduct a broad cultural critique of the imperial mode of
living,
(2) help plan for a structural shift toward small farming activi-
ties in the agribusiness sector,
(3) select at least six potential ethiotopian projects, and
(4) prepare implementation plans for these selected projects. The
Mission essentially asked "where can we plant more teff and pro-
mote the spirit of the mesob (public wealth)?"
```

America needs Ethiopian economic advisors to blanket America* with injera, a sponge-like pancake made from teff, the new super food that used to be banned.

It will be like Borges's map Baudrillard famously describes in *Simulacra and Simulation*, "a map so detailed that it ends up covering the territory exactly."

And so a map made of injera, what would that mean? Well, for one, to compliment the injera, it would have to be an America of many *watts* (the Ethiopian and Eritrean stew or curry prepared with chicken, beef, lamb, or vegetables, seasoned with spice mixtures such as *berbere* and *niter kibbeh*, a seasoned clarified butter).

It will also mean we eat with our hands, not stabbing at the food with our neoliberal knives and forks, as Roland Barthes points out in *Mythologies*.

We will hold gently the injera in our hands and gently scoop up the offering (watt, tibs, shiro, fosolia, goman, tikel and so on) and lovingly maneuver the little packet into our mouths and then go back for more, tearing off a piece of injera, etcetera, lovingly. Conversation and laughter abounding. We will sit around a basket-like table (*mesob*), made of woven straw dyed with reds, yellows, oranges, purples, greens, blues, on wooden, three-legged stools (*barchuma*), eating from a communal plate (*gebeta*) with our hands, you there to my left, you there to my right, kin to kin to kin, our hands together in the food.

> Radio Ethiopia: "My brother, don't be like a hollow seed."

Sources *(In order of their appearance)*

Ethiopian Numbers 1-7: "Ge'ez is an ancient Semitic language with its own script originated around the 5th century BC." Metaferia, *Metaappz*. https://www.metaappz.com/References/AmharicAndGeezNumbersReferenceTable.aspx

Amharic Proverbs: William H. Armstrong and Fisseha Demoz Gebre Egzi, trans. "Amharic Mandy," *Ethiopia Observer* (Vol. XII, No. 1). May 22, 1969.

Alain Borer, *Rimbaud in Abyssinia*. Trans. Rosemarie Waldrop. New York: William Murrow, 1984.

Jack Spicer, *The Collected Books of Jack Spicer*. Robin Blaser, ed. Black Sparrow Books, 1975.

Harold Pinter. "Nobel Lecture: Art, Truth, and Politics." Nobelprize.org (2005).
   The stanza beginning with "*It never happened*" samples Pinter's "Nobel Lecture": "The United States supported and in many cases engendered every right wing military dictatorship in the world after the end of the Second World War. I refer to Indonesia, Greece, Uruguay, Brazil, Paraguay, Haiti, Turkey, the Philippines, Guatemala, El Salvador, and, of course, Chile. The horror the United States inflicted upon Chile in 1973 can never be purged and can never be forgiven.
   Hundreds of thousands of deaths took place throughout these countries. Did they take place? And are they in all cases attributable to US foreign policy? The answer is yes they did take place and they are attributable to American foreign policy. But you wouldn't know it.
   It never happened. Nothing ever happened. Even while it was happening it wasn't happening. It didn't matter. It was of no interest. The crimes of the United States have been systematic, constant, vicious, remorseless, but very few people have actually talked about them. You have to hand it to America. It has exercised a quite clinical manipulation of power worldwide while masquerading as a force for universal good. It's a brilliant, even witty, highly successful act of hypnosis."

Faye Dayi. Directed by Jessica Bashir, produced by Doha Film Institute, 2021.
"Dream of rimbaud." www.oceanstar.com/patti/bio/rimbaud.htm

Joe Brainard, *I Remember*. Granary Books, 2001 (first published 1970).

Susan Williams, *White Malice: The CIA and the Covert Recolonization of Africa*. Public Affairs, 2021.

John Perkins, *Confessions of an Economic Hitman*. Penguin, 2005.

Asayehgn Desta, *From Economic Dependency and Stagnation to Democratic Development State*. Red Sea Press, 2014.

Hubert Humphrey. http://www.great-quotes.com/quotes/author/Hubert/Humphrey

Acknowledgments

Excerpts from "My Book About Ethiopia" were published in *The Claudius App* (2012).

I am grateful to Kit Sibert and Tim Whitsel for critiquing the manuscript, as well as the other members of our writing group "Poetry 1"—Karen McPherson, Cecelia Hagen, Kelly Terwilliger, and Anita Sullivan—who critiqued versions of the poems. I also appreciate the hosts of the local reading series in Eugene and Springfield for the opportunity to air the work in public: Joan Dobbie (River Road Reading Series), Carter McKenzie and Jenny Root (Springfield Reading Series), Toni Hanner and Sam Roxas Chua (Windfall Reading Series). Special thanks goes to Chris Alexander for nudging me to write about my struggle to write *Radio Ethiopia*—"write about that"—when we were in Buffalo.

Posthumous thanks to my parents for the best education anyone can hope for in the form of travel, and for my dear traveling companions, Becky and our two younger brothers Mike and Paul. Your memory will always be with us.

Love to Tammy and Nora for their unwavering support through the years.

And, finally, thanks so much to Michael Tsegaye for the cover's wonderful photograph and for the book design, and to Tod Thilleman at Spuyten Duyvil for providing my work a home.

www.ingramcontent.com/pod-product-compliance
Lightning Source LLC
LaVergne TN
LVHW060135080526
838202LV00050B/4123